INSIDE THE
NFL

DALLAS
COWBOYS

BY TODD RYAN

SportsZone
An Imprint of Abdo Publishing
abdobooks.com

abdobooks.com

Published by Abdo Publishing, a division of ABDO, PO Box 398166, Minneapolis, Minnesota 55439. Copyright © 2020 by Abdo Consulting Group, Inc. International copyrights reserved in all countries. No part of this book may be reproduced in any form without written permission from the publisher. SportsZone™ is a trademark and logo of Abdo Publishing.

Printed in the United States of America, North Mankato, Minnesota
042019
092019

THIS BOOK CONTAINS
RECYCLED MATERIALS

Cover Photo: Jim Cowsert/AP Images
Interior Photos: Focus on Sport/Getty Images, 5; NFL Photos/AP Images, 7, 29; Tony Tomsic/AP Images, 8, 10, 17, 19, 43; Walter Iooss Jr./Sports Illustrated/Set Number: X12884/Getty Images, 13; David Durochik/AP Images, 15; AP Images, 21; Ron Heflin/AP Images, 24; Glenn James/AP Images, 27; Tim Sharp/AP Images, 31; Tony Gutierrez/AP Images, 35; Scott Boehm/AP Images, 36; Kevin Terrell/AP Images, 41

Editor: Patrick Donnelly
Series Designer: Craig Hinton

Library of Congress Control Number: 2018965787

Publisher's Cataloging-in-Publication Data

Names: Ryan, Todd, author.
Title: Dallas Cowboys / by Todd Ryan
Description: Minneapolis, Minnesota: Abdo Publishing, 2020 | Series: Inside the NFL | Includes online resources and index.
Identifiers: ISBN 9781532118449 (lib. bdg.) | ISBN 9781532172625 (ebook) | ISBN 9781644941041 (pbk.)
Subjects: LCSH: Dallas Cowboys (Football team)--Juvenile literature. | National Football League --Juvenile literature. | Football teams--Juvenile literature. | American football--Juvenile literature.
Classification: DDC 796.33264--dc23

TABLE OF
CONTENTS

CHAPTER 1

CHAMPIONS AT LAST

The Dallas Cowboys were one of the top teams in the National Football League (NFL) from 1966 through 1970. The team was an amazing 52–16–2 in the regular season during that span. But when it came to winning in the playoffs, the Cowboys struggled. Dallas lost to Green Bay in the NFL Championship Game in both 1966 and 1967. They lost to the Cleveland Browns in the divisional round the next two years.

Cowboys fans believed their team was finally going to break through in 1970. The Cowboys finished the regular season 10–4. Then they won two playoff games and advanced to Super Bowl V against the Baltimore Colts. But the Cowboys again failed to end their championship drought. The Colts kicked a field goal in the final minute to win 16–13.

Dallas quarterback Craig Morton drops back to pass against the Baltimore Colts in Super Bowl V.

TAKING CHARGE

Craig Morton was the Cowboys' starting quarterback at the beginning of the 1971 season. But midway through the season, Roger Staubach took over. Including the postseason, Staubach won nine straight games to lead the Cowboys to their first NFL title.

The loss was tough for the Cowboys to take. That disappointment seemed to carry into the start of the 1971 season. After winning their first two games, the Cowboys then lost three of their next five. Dallas had a 4–3 record halfway through the season.

But the Cowboys started to turn their season around. On November 7 they beat the St. Louis Cardinals 16–13. That sparked a seven-game winning streak. The Cowboys finished the regular season 11–3. They went on to beat the Minnesota Vikings 20–12 in the first round of the playoffs. Then they beat the San Francisco 49ers 14–3 in the National Football Conference (NFC) Championship Game. They advanced to their second straight Super Bowl.

Super Bowl VI was in New Orleans. The Cowboys' opponent was the American Football Conference (AFC) champion Miami Dolphins. Dallas fans were nervous before the game. They had seen their team come up short in too many title games before.

✕ Quarterback Roger Staubach scrambles past a Miami Dolphins defender during Super Bowl VI.

But this Cowboys team proved to be like no other before. From the start of the game, the Cowboys dominated the Dolphins.

Dallas' offense racked up 23 first downs in the game. It gained 352 yards. The defense held Miami to only 10 first downs and 185 total yards. Dallas never trailed in the game.

Dallas running back Duane Thomas fights off a Dolphins defender during Super Bowl VI.

The Cowboys jumped out to a 3–0 lead at the end of the first quarter and held a 10–3 lead at the half. They added a touchdown in the third and another one in the fourth quarter. Meanwhile, the defense kept the clamps on the Dolphins. The Cowboys won 24–3. Years of playoff frustrations were over.

Leading the charge for the Cowboys on offense were quarterback Roger Staubach and running back Duane Thomas. Staubach ran the offense to near perfection. He completed 12 of his 19 passes for 119 yards and two touchdowns. He earned the Super Bowl Most Valuable Player (MVP) Award. Meanwhile, Thomas slashed his way through the Miami offense for 95 rushing yards and a touchdown on 19 carries.

But the offense was only half the story. It was the Cowboys' defense that shut down the Miami offense all day. The Dolphins became the first team to not score a touchdown in the Super Bowl.

HONORING HOWLEY

Chuck Howley was the oldest player on the Cowboys' roster in 1971. He was playing in his eleventh season with the team. In 1977 Howley was inducted into the Cowboys Ring of Honor. He joined an elite group of former Dallas players, coaches, and executives whose names and numbers appeared on the blue ring that separates the upper and lower decks at Texas Stadium and now at AT&T Stadium.

Cowboys coach Tom Landry is carried off the field after Dallas defeated the Miami Dolphins 24–3 in Super Bowl VI.

Linebacker Chuck Howley and defensive tackle Bob Lilly were the stars. Lilly completely dominated Miami's offensive line. He even recorded a sack of Miami quarterback Bob Griese for a Super Bowl–record 29-yard loss in the first quarter.

Howley was even more effective. He recovered a fumble in the first quarter to set up a Cowboys field goal. He added an interception in the fourth quarter that he returned 41 yards. That led to a Staubach touchdown pass to tight end Mike Ditka for the game's final score.

The Cowboys were finally champions. The team could forget about its challenging first six years as a franchise from 1960 to 1965. Instead, the Cowboys were on the verge of becoming known as "America's Team."

MR. COWBOY

Bob Lilly was a seven-time All-Pro for the Cowboys. He was also the first player inducted into the team's Ring of Honor. During the pregame ceremony in 1975, Tom Landry described Lilly as "the greatest player I've ever coached." The Cowboys don't officially retire numbers, but no Cowboy has worn Lilly's No. 74 since he retired.

CHAPTER 2

AMERICA'S TEAM

The Dallas Cowboys came into existence on January 28, 1960. That is when the NFL awarded an expansion franchise to Clint Murchison Jr. and Bedford Wynne. Murchison was the majority owner. The team was first known as the Steers and then the Rangers before the owners settled on the Cowboys.

The Cowboys had only a few months to put a team together before their first game that fall. Murchison, however, had already lined up some key leadership off the field. The most notable were general manager Tex Schramm, director of player personnel Gil Brandt, and head coach Tom Landry. All three would remain in those positions for the next 29 years.

The Cowboys stocked their roster through an expansion draft. During that draft, they selected three players off

Linebacker Chuck Howley (54) anchored the Cowboys defense throughout the 1960s.

the rosters of each of the existing 12 NFL teams. The rest of the roster was pieced together by signing free agents and through trades with other teams. They were able to trade their future draft picks as well as the players they already obtained. However, the Cowboys were not able to build through the NFL Draft. They entered the league too late to participate.

Except for a few players, the team was short on talent. That showed on the field. The Cowboys did not win a game their first season, going 0–11–1. In fact, the team would struggle to win at all during its first five years of existence. Its best record was 5–8–1, which they managed in both 1962 and 1964.

Under the steady leadership of Schramm, Brandt, and Landry, Dallas slowly added talented players. Quarterback Don Meredith and running back Don Perkins arrived in 1960. Then the Cowboys added defensive tackle Bob Lilly and linebacker Chuck Howley in 1961, and linebacker Lee Roy Jordan in 1963. Finally, the Cowboys drafted

ALL ABOUT THE NAME

When Clint Murchison was trying to come up with a team name, his first selection was the Steers. He then chose the Dallas Rangers. That was the same nickname as the minor league franchise that was expected to leave the city. However, the Rangers never left and so Murchison settled on Cowboys.

Cowboys quarterback Don Meredith barks out the signals in a game against Washington.

quarterback Roger Staubach, defensive back Mel Renfro, and wide receiver Bob Hayes in 1964.

Still, the Cowboys' record over their first five years was 18–46–4. That finally began to change in 1965. With loads of young but talented players, Dallas went 7–7. The Cowboys would not experience another losing season until 1986.

CAPTAIN COMEBACK

The Cowboys selected quarterback Roger Staubach in the tenth round of the 1964 NFL Draft. Though he'd won the Heisman Trophy at the US Naval Academy, a five-year postgraduate commitment to the Navy scared off most teams. Staubach finally arrived in Dallas in 1969. Over the next decade, he would lead the Cowboys to one of the greatest stretches of success that any franchise has ever experienced.

Staubach was a Pro Bowl selection six times and NFL passing champion four times. He guided the Cowboys to two Super Bowl titles and was named the MVP of Super Bowl VI. He also ranks third in club history with 22,700 yards passing.

He became known as "Captain Comeback." That was because he led 23 game-winning drives. One of his most famous passes was a 50-yard "Hail Mary" touchdown pass to Drew Pearson in the 1975 playoffs to defeat the Minnesota Vikings. Staubach retired after the 1979 season and was enshrined in the Pro Football Hall of Fame in 1985.

The Cowboys also qualified for the playoffs 17 times in 18 years from 1966 through 1983.

Meredith was leading the offense in 1966. The Cowboys won their first Eastern Conference title that season. However, they lost to the Green Bay Packers 34–27 in the NFL Championship Game. Dallas advanced to the NFL Championship Game again in 1967 and again lost to Green Bay,

✕ Cowboys running back Tony Dorsett (33) ran for 66 yards and a touchdown as a rookie in Super Bowl XII.

this time 21–17. That game is now known as the "Ice Bowl" because it was played in below-zero temperatures on a frozen field in Green Bay, Wisconsin.

From 1966 to 1969, the Cowboys went 42–12–2. And they were only getting warmed up. During the 1970s, Dallas went to five Super Bowls. The Cowboys lost the Super Bowl after the

1970 season to the Baltimore Colts and after the 1975 and 1978 seasons to the Pittsburgh Steelers. But they won the title after the 1971 season against the Miami Dolphins and after the 1977 season against the Denver Broncos.

Leading the charge in the 1970s was a collection of future Hall of Fame players. They included Staubach and running back Tony Dorsett. Both players starred when the Cowboys beat the Broncos 27–10 in Super Bowl XII. Staubach led the way, completing 17 of 25 passes for 183 yards. The rookie Dorsett scored the game's first touchdown. Despite having to leave in the third quarter with an injury, he still ran for 66 yards on 15 carries.

The Cowboys' defense had shut down opposing offenses all season. That is just what they did to Denver in the Super Bowl. Led by safety Cliff Harris and defensive tackle Randy White, the defense was one of the best throughout the 1970s. In Super Bowl XII, the Cowboys limited the Broncos to 156 total yards.

The Cowboys were on top of the NFL world during the 1970s. After the 1978 season, NFL Films was putting together a highlight video. The film crew wanted a catchy name for the video, so editor-in-chief Bob Ryan called the Cowboys

Cowboys defensive end Ed "Too Tall" Jones lowers the boom on former teammate and Broncos quarterback Craig Morton in Super Bowl XII.

"America's Team." It is a nickname that has stayed with the team to this day.

However, after their long run of success in the 1970s, it would be a while before the Cowboys could again live up to their lofty nickname.

CHAPTER 3

FALLING ON HARD TIMES

After their Super Bowl XIII loss to Pittsburgh, the Cowboys did not return to the Super Bowl for 14 years. The franchise underwent a lot of change during the 1980s. One of the biggest changes came in 1984 when Clint Murchison Jr. sold the team to H. R. "Bum" Bright. Only five years later, Bright sold the team to Jerry Jones.

In 1980 Danny White took over at quarterback for the retired Roger Staubach. Dallas finished 12–4 in each of his first two seasons. The Cowboys went 6–3 in the strike-shortened 1982 season. In 1983 White again led the Cowboys to a 12–4 record. But White didn't get the Cowboys to the Super Bowl. Because of that, he never won the hearts of the Dallas fans in the way that Staubach did. In 10 playoff

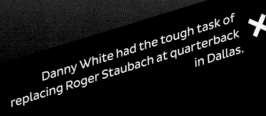

Danny White had the tough task of replacing Roger Staubach at quarterback in Dallas.

TONY DORSETT

Tony Dorsett finished his career with 12,739 yards and was a four-time Pro Bowl selection. His most famous run came on January 3, 1983, at Minnesota. He took a handoff from Danny White and raced 99 yards for a touchdown. That set an NFL record that can be matched but can never be broken. Dorsett entered the Pro Football Hall of Fame in 1994.

games from 1980 to 1985, White's Cowboys were only 5–5.

The 1985 season was the last winning season for legendary head coach Tom Landry. The Cowboys dropped to 7–9 in 1986. It was their first losing season since 1964. The following year Dallas went 7–8. Then the Cowboys collapsed. In 1988 they suffered their worst season since 1960 as they fell to a woeful 3–13.

Landry had been the only head coach the Cowboys ever had. But Jones fired him after the 1988 season. Jones made it clear that he was in charge. He hired Jimmy Johnson to replace Landry without Schramm knowing.

Seeing that he was no longer welcome, Tex Schramm retired. Gil Brandt stayed a little longer to help with the upcoming draft. But soon after that, Brandt was gone as well. In a matter of months, three people who had been cornerstones of the franchise were no longer members of the Dallas Cowboys.

COACH LANDRY

For 29 years, Tom Landry was the only head coach the Dallas Cowboys had ever known. During that time, he had a record of 270–178–6 (including playoffs). Only three head coaches have won more NFL games.

As an assistant coach for the New York Giants in the 1950s, Landry helped develop the 4–3 defense. That scheme used four down linemen and three linebackers. Many teams still use that formation today. As Dallas's head coach, Landry introduced offensive motion, popularized the shotgun formation, used situational substitutions, and created the flex defense.

Jones's handling of Landry, Brandt, and Schramm was unpopular in Dallas. But Jones had a plan, and he was going to stick with it. Johnson had been a successful coach at the University of Miami. Both Johnson and Jones shared the same vision. They believed that it was time for a change. It was out with the old and in with the new.

One of the new players was wide receiver Michael Irvin. The team had drafted Irvin in 1988. Despite Irvin's contributions (32 catches, 654 yards, five touchdowns), the Cowboys still finished with the worst record in the league in his rookie season. That meant they had the first pick in the 1989

Cowboys owner Jerry Jones, shown in 1995, bought the team in 1989. He fired head coach Tom Landry shortly after.

NFL Draft. Jones and Johnson wanted a new leader. They also wanted a player who they felt could take advantage of Irvin's talents. The player they targeted was quarterback Troy Aikman. That selection helped return the Cowboys to glory.

TEX SCHRAMM

Earnest "Tex" Schramm joined the Cowboys as the team's first president and general manager. Dallas went to five Super Bowls and compiled an NFL-record 20 straight winning seasons during his time. Schramm's influence was felt throughout the league. He helped establish the traditional Cowboys home game each Thanksgiving Day. His support led to the use of instant replay to help officials during games. Schramm was also part of creating the wild-card playoff system. He even created the Dallas Cowboys Cheerleaders, who were the first of their kind in professional football.

The Jimmy Johnson era did not start well in Dallas. Relying heavily on a group of young players, the Cowboys went 1–15. Their only win came at Washington on November 5.

The team made a decision midway through the 1989 season that would dramatically change its course. When it was clear that the Cowboys were not going to be title contenders, Jones arranged a trade that would send star running back Herschel Walker to the Minnesota Vikings. In return, the Cowboys would receive several high draft picks spread over three years.

The trade was supposed to put the Vikings over the top by giving them a star player. Instead, it was the Cowboys who came out ahead—way ahead.

CHAPTER 4

THE TRIPLETS

After trading Herschel Walker, the Cowboys used the draft picks they got to build a new core of stars. Some of the players they selected with those picks were running back Emmitt Smith, defensive tackle Russell Maryland, cornerback Kevin Smith, strong safety Darren Woodson, and cornerback Clayton Holmes.

The addition of Emmitt Smith to Troy Aikman and Michael Irvin helped turn the Cowboys into an offensive power. The three players soon became known as "the Triplets." The vastly improved team finished 7–9 in 1990. The Cowboys would improve even more in the years to come.

With Aikman, Smith, and Irvin, the Cowboys soon dominated the league. In 1991 they went 11–5 and were back in the playoffs for the first time in six years. They finished

Troy Aikman took over as the Cowboys' starting quarterback during his rookie season in 1989.

ROBO QB

Troy Aikman's professional career did not get off to a great start. He was thrown into the Cowboys' lineup as a rookie in 1989. Aikman lost his first 11 games and Dallas went 1–15. But Aikman would go on to become one of the greatest quarterbacks the franchise has ever seen.

He guided the Cowboys to four straight appearances in the NFC Championship Game and won three Super Bowl titles. He won 90 games during the 1990s, becoming the winningest quarterback of any decade.

By the time he retired, Aikman racked up 47 different team passing records. They included completions (2,898), passing yards (32,942), and touchdown passes (165). Aikman was selected to six straight Pro Bowls. He was inducted into the Pro Football Hall of Fame in 2006. After his playing days were over, Aikman went on to a successful broadcasting career.

the 1992 season 13–3. After two more victories, the Cowboys were back in the Super Bowl. Aikman was named the game's MVP after throwing four touchdown passes as the Cowboys demolished the Buffalo Bills 52–17 in Super Bowl XXVII.

The Cowboys were back one year later. They had cruised to a 12–4 regular-season record. After two playoff victories, they met the Bills again in Super Bowl XXVIII. The results were similar to those from the year before. Smith ran for 132 yards

Emmitt Smith was the final piece of the puzzle for the Cowboys' explosive offensive attack.

and two touchdowns to earn MVP honors. The Cowboys beat the Bills 30–13.

"It's too early to call us the 'Team of the Nineties,'" Aikman said after the game. "But I guess this says last year was not

DUAL THREATS

Emmitt Smith was a star running back at the University of Florida. But many pro scouts did not believe he was big enough to handle the punishment that NFL running backs receive. It's safe to say he proved them wrong. After 15 years in the NFL—13 of which were with Dallas—Smith retired as the league's career rushing leader with 18,355 yards and 164 touchdowns. He was inducted into the Pro Football Hall of Fame in 2010.

Michael Irvin retired after the 1999 season due to a spine injury. He left the Cowboys owning or sharing 20 team receiving records. They included career receptions (750), career yardage (11,904), and 100-yard receiving games (47). When he retired, only two NFL receivers had more 1,000-yard receiving seasons than Irvin's seven. In 1995, Irvin had at least 100 receiving yards in 11 games, an NFL record that was tied by Detroit's Calvin Johnson in 2012. He was inducted into the Pro Football Hall of Fame in 2007.

a fluke. It puts us with some great teams. What exactly that means to all of us, I'm not sure."

Aikman, Smith, and Irvin were spectacular during Dallas's back-to-back title seasons. Aikman threw for a combined 6,545 yards in the two seasons, including 38 touchdowns and only 20 interceptions. He completed 69.1 percent of his passes in 1993. Smith led the NFL in rushing from 1991 to 1993 and again in 1995. That included a 1,713-yard, 18-touchdown season

From left, Troy Aikman, Emmitt Smith, and Michael Irvin were known as "the Triplets."

in 1992. Meanwhile, Irvin had five straight seasons with more than 1,000 receiving yards (1991 to 1995). He averaged nearly 90 catches and more than 1,400 yards per season in that span.

Johnson had a falling out with Jones after the 1993 season. That led to Johnson resigning as the team's coach. Jones brought in former University of Oklahoma head coach

Barry Switzer. Thanks in large part to the Triplets, the Cowboys hardly missed a beat.

Dallas went 12–4 during Switzer's first season in 1994. But they were denied a chance to win their third straight Super Bowl. The Cowboys lost to the San Francisco 49ers 38–28 in the NFC Championship Game.

However, they were back again one year later. The Cowboys went 12–4 in the regular season. This time, they reached the Super Bowl, where they defeated the Pittsburgh Steelers 27–17.

Cornerback Larry Brown had a big game for Dallas. He came away with two interceptions. He returned his first interception 44 yards to the Pittsburgh 18. That set up Smith's 1-yard touchdown run to give the Cowboys a 20–7 lead.

The second came in the fourth quarter and helped the Cowboys seal the win. The Steelers had cut the deficit to 20–17.

PRIME TIME

Dallas signed Deion Sanders before the 1995 season. Sanders was a star cornerback. But he also played wide receiver at times and returned kicks and punts. Sanders also played for four different Major League Baseball teams. He even played in the 1992 World Series with the Atlanta Braves. Sanders helped the Cowboys win Super Bowl XXX. He played in Dallas from 1995 to 1999 and was known as one of the top defensive players in the league.

But Brown came up with another interception. He returned it 33 yards to set up Smith's 4-yard touchdown run.

That capped an amazing four-year run by the team. Switzer lasted only two more seasons with Dallas. He was fired in 1997 after the team went 6–10. Steelers offensive coordinator Chan Gailey was hired to try to lift the Cowboys back to the Super Bowl. But he lasted only two seasons.

Jones promoted defensive coordinator Dave Campo to the head coach role in 2000. But age caught up to the Cowboys. Many of the key players that lifted Dallas to three Super Bowl titles in the 1990s were gone or close to retirement.

Irvin retired after the 1999 season. Aikman's last season came in 2000. Smith was still a key member of the team. But he was no longer the dominant running back he had been five years earlier. The loss of talent on the field showed in the standings. The Cowboys were 5–11 in Campo's first season.

The Cowboys struggled to find a replacement for Aikman. They posted 5–11 records during each of the next two seasons as well. The core of the team that dominated in the 1990s was almost all gone, as was Campo after the 2002 season.

CHAPTER 5

TRYING TO GET BACK

One of the few highlights in 2002 came on October 27. The Cowboys were playing the Seattle Seahawks at Texas Stadium. On an 11-yard run that day, Emmitt Smith became the NFL's all-time leading rusher. He moved past Walter Payton's mark of 16,726 career rushing yards. Smith finished the day with 109 yards on 24 carries.

After the 2002 season, Cowboys owner Jerry Jones named Bill Parcells the team's new head coach. Parcells had won two Super Bowls with the New York Giants. He quickly turned the Cowboys around. Parcells showed faith in Quincy Carter in 2003. The young quarterback responded by throwing for 3,302 yards and 17 touchdowns. Carter led Dallas to a 10–6

Emmitt Smith rejoices after breaking the NFL career rushing record in October 2002.

Tony Romo was a surprise star when he took over at quarterback in 2006.

record, the team's first winning season since 1998. But the Cowboys again lost in the first round of the playoffs.

Dallas took a step backward in 2004. The Cowboys went 6–10 as the quarterback carousel continued. Carter lost his job

AN UNLIKELY STAR

Tony Romo played his college football at Division II Eastern Illinois University. No teams took a chance on him in the NFL Draft. The Cowboys instead signed him as a free agent.

Romo was a backup for his first two and a half seasons. He did not start until October 29, 2006, against Carolina. By the end of the year, his performance had been so impressive that he became Dallas's first Pro Bowl quarterback since Troy Aikman a decade earlier. In 2007 he guided the Cowboys to a 13–3 record, tying the franchise record for most regular-season wins.

Romo retired in 2017 and held multiple team records at the time including most passing touchdowns and passing yards. He quickly found another career as he became a successful game analyst on NFL television broadcasts.

to veteran Vinny Testaverde. The new quarterback threw for 3,532 yards and 17 touchdowns. But Testaverde lasted only one season. Drew Bledsoe was brought in to lead the team in 2005. He threw for 3,639 yards and 23 touchdowns. But Dallas went 9–7 and failed to make the playoffs.

Bledsoe began the 2006 season as the starter. However, Parcells switched to undrafted and untested Tony Romo midway through. With Romo leading the offense, the Cowboys won six of their final 10 games. They ended the year with a 9–7 record and a spot in the playoffs.

The Cowboys lost again in the wild-card game. But the future finally looked bright for the team. Romo threw for 2,903 yards and 19 touchdowns in his 12 games. He blossomed in 2007. Romo threw for 4,211 yards and 36 touchdowns to lead Dallas to a 13–3 record in coach Wade Phillips' first year.

Romo continued his impressive play the next two seasons. In 2008, he threw for 3,448 yards and 26 touchdowns in only 13 games. Then he threw for 4,483 yards and 26 touchdowns with only nine interceptions in 2009. The Cowboys went 11–5 and won the NFC Eastern Division title. The Cowboys finally won a first-round playoff game, too. They beat the Philadelphia Eagles 34–14 in the wild-card game. It was their first postseason win since 1996. That was as far as the Cowboys would go in 2009, however. They lost

A NEW HOME

In 2009 the Cowboys opened their new $1.2-billion stadium. They had played in Texas Stadium for 38 seasons. Their new home is one of the largest domed structures in the world. It features a retractable roof as well as massive high-definition TV screens that hang over the center of the field.

to the Vikings and their star quarterback, Brett Favre, in the second round.

From 2010 to 2013, Romo and the Dallas offense continued to shine. However, injuries led to a 6–10 showing in 2010. The next three seasons brought their own special form of frustration. Each year the Cowboys had a chance to clinch a playoff spot with a victory in Week 17. Each year they lost.

The most memorable of those defeats might have been in 2013. In Week 16, Romo had led a late comeback to defeat Washington 24–23. However, Romo injured his back late in the game and couldn't play in Week 17 as Dallas faced Philadelphia. Journeyman backup Kyle Orton stepped in and had success throwing to tight end Jason Witten and wide receiver Dez Bryant. But Orton threw a late interception and the Cowboys lost 24–22. The Eagles went to the playoffs and the Cowboys stayed home.

Romo returned in 2014 and Dallas got over the hump. The Cowboys went 12–4 and won their division as Romo, Bryant, and Witten spearheaded the fifth-best scoring offense in the NFL. They slipped past the Detroit Lions in the first round of the playoffs. Then it was on to Green Bay for a divisional playoff game against the Packers.

The Cowboys led 14–10 at halftime and stayed close to favored Green Bay for the entire game. Late in the game, Dallas trailed 26–21. On fourth-and-2, the Cowboys decided to have Romo throw a long pass to Bryant. It looked as if Bryant made the catch at the 1-yard line before lunging toward the goal line, where the ball popped out of his hands. After a video review, the officials said Bryant had not controlled the ball all the way through the process of making the catch. They ruled the pass incomplete. It was a controversial finish and more heartbreak for Dallas.

Romo played only five more NFL games before retiring due to his back injuries. He was replaced by rookie quarterback Dak Prescott, whom the Cowboys selected late in the fourth round of the 2016 NFL Draft. Prescott started alongside running back Ezekiel Elliott, their 2016 first-round pick. The two thrived in their first season in the NFL. The Cowboys lost to the Giants

AN UNLIKELY TANDEM

The Cowboys drafted Ezekiel Elliott in the first round of the 2016 NFL Draft with the idea that he would be a good running back to play next to quarterback Tony Romo. Just before the season, however, things changed. Romo was injured and Elliott found himself playing alongside fellow rookie Dak Prescott. The move ended up being a major success as Dallas went 13–3 and scored the fifth-most points in the NFL that season.

✗ Ezekiel Elliott dives into the end zone to score his first NFL touchdown against the New York Giants in 2016.

in Week 1 but then won their next 11 games. Dallas finished 13–3 and once again matched up with the Packers in the playoffs, only to lose on a last-second field goal.

Prescott and Elliott led the Cowboys to records of 9–7 and 10–6 over the next two years. The 2018 squad won the NFC East and defeated the Seattle Seahawks in a wild-card playoff game. Despite their struggles trying to get back to the top, the Cowboys and their fans believe there is still a chance they can return to their Super Bowl–winning days as America's Team.

TIMELINE

The Dallas Cowboys enter the NFL on January 28.

1960

Dallas finishes 7–7, the first time it did not have a losing record since entering the league.

1965

The Cowboys finish 10–3–1 and win the Eastern Conference title but lose to Green Bay in the NFL title game.

1966

Dallas goes 10–4 and wins the NFC title, earning the right to represent the new NFC in the Super Bowl.

1970

Baltimore defeats the Cowboys 16–13 to win the Super Bowl on January 17.

1971

The Cowboys win their first Super Bowl title, defeating Miami 24–3 on January 16.

1972

Dallas loses to the Pittsburgh Steelers, 21–17, in Super Bowl X on January 18.

1976

The Cowboys shut down the Denver Broncos, 27–10, to win Super Bowl XII on January 15.

1978

Pittsburgh defeats the Cowboys once again in the Super Bowl, edging Dallas 35–31 on January 21.

1979

After a 3–13 season, Tom Landry is fired by new team owner Jerry Jones.

1988

The Cowboys win their third Super Bowl title, defeating Buffalo 52–17 in Super Bowl XXVII on January 31.

1993

The Cowboys repeat as Super Bowl champions on January 30, again beating Buffalo, this time by a score of 30–13.

1994

The Cowboys win their third Super Bowl title in four years on January 28, beating Pittsburgh 27–17.

1996

Dave Campo is named the new coach, replacing Chan Gailey, who coached the team for only two years.

2000

Troy Aikman announces his retirement on April 9 after 12 years with the Cowboys.

2001

Emmitt Smith bursts up the middle on an 11–yard run against the Seahawks to become the NFL's all-time leading rusher.

2002

The Cowboys move into their new home, the $1.2 billion Cowboys Stadium.

2009

DeMarco Murray rushes for a team record 1,845 yards as the Cowboys go 12–4 and win the division for the first time in five years.

2014

Due to an injury to Tony Romo, rookie Dak Prescott takes over as the Cowboys' starting quarterback and leads the team to a 13–3 record.

2016

Ezekiel Elliott leads the Cowboys to a division title with 1,434 rushing yards.

2018

QUICK STATS

FRANCHISE HISTORY

1960–

SUPER BOWLS
(wins in bold)

1970 (V), **1971 (VI)**, 1975 (X), **1977 (XII)**, 1978 (XIII), **1992 (XXVII)**, **1993 (XXVIII)**, **1995 (XXX)**

NFC CHAMPIONSHIP GAMES *(since 1970 AFL-NFL merger)*

1970, 1971, 1972, 1973, 1975, 1977, 1978, 1980, 1981, 1982, 1992, 1993, 1994, 1995

KEY COACHES

Jason Garrett (2010–): 77–59, 2–3 (playoffs)
Jimmy Johnson (1989–93): 44–36, 7–1 (playoffs)
Tom Landry (1960–88): 250–162–6, 20–16 (playoffs)

KEY PLAYERS
(position, seasons with team)

Troy Aikman (QB, 1989–2000)
Dez Bryant (WR, 2010–17)
Tony Dorsett (RB, 1977–87)
Ezekiel Elliott (RB, 2016–)
Bob Hayes (WR, 1965–74)
Chuck Howley (LB, 1961–73)
Michael Irvin (WR, 1988–99)
Bob Lilly (DT, 1961–74)
Dak Prescott (QB, 2016–)
Mel Renfro (DB, 1964–77)
Tony Romo (QB, 2004–16)
Emmitt Smith (RB, 1990–2002)
Roger Staubach (QB, 1969–79)
DeMarcus Ware (LB, 2005–13)
Randy White (DT, 1975–88)
Jason Witten (TE, 2003–17)
Rayfield Wright (T/TE, 1967–79)

HOME FIELDS

AT&T Stadium (2009–)
    Also known as
    Cowboys Stadium
Texas Stadium (1971–2008)
Cotton Bowl (1960–71)

*All statistics through 2018 season

QUOTES AND ANECDOTES

"Tony Dorsett made a big difference when he came in '77. Getting Dorsett was a real shot in the arm. This guy was a sensational player. He had speed, he was tough, could run inside. He took a lot of pressure off me. With him we had a very balanced game. That year Tony Hill also came, and when you have Tony and Drew [Pearson] and Tony, we were one heck of an offense."

—Roger Staubach

AT&T Stadium wowed a lot of fans when it opened in 2009. Its greatest feature might be the large scoreboard hung from the ceiling in the center of the field. It weighs 600 tons (544 metric tons) and the display is equal to 3,268 52-inch (132 cm) televisions. When it debuted, it was recognized as the world's largest video display.

"I was thinking about quitting coaching altogether and going into business. When Clint and Tex called, I told my wife, 'Well, we might as well take a shot.' The thing was, I wasn't so sure that the Cowboys were going to last more than a couple of years in Dallas. I lived here, and Dallas was a city that didn't turn out unless you won. If you didn't win [the fans] said, 'We'll go do something else.' And I knew we wouldn't win for a while as an expansion team. But it came down to figuring. 'Why not just take a shot?'"

—Tom Landry, explaining his thought process when he was asked by owner Clint Murchison and general manager Tex Schramm to become the first head coach of the Cowboys.

GLOSSARY

comeback
When a team losing a game rallies to tie the score or take the lead.

dominant
Proving to be consistently better than an opponent.

draft
A system that allows teams to acquire new players coming into a league.

expansion
The addition of new teams to increase the size of a league.

flex defense
A defensive system in which the defensive linemen line up in different areas based on the opponent's alignment.

free agent
A player whose rights are not owned by any team.

Hail Mary
A long and high pass thrown out of desperation to try to score a touchdown; usually takes place at the end of a half.

legendary
Generally regarded as one of the best to ever play.

offensive motion
When one or more players shift their position before a play starts, either by taking a few steps to one side or the other or running to the other side of the field.

rookie
A professional athlete in his or her first year of competition.

shotgun
A formation in which the quarterback lines up 3 or 5 yards behind the center and takes the snap in the air.